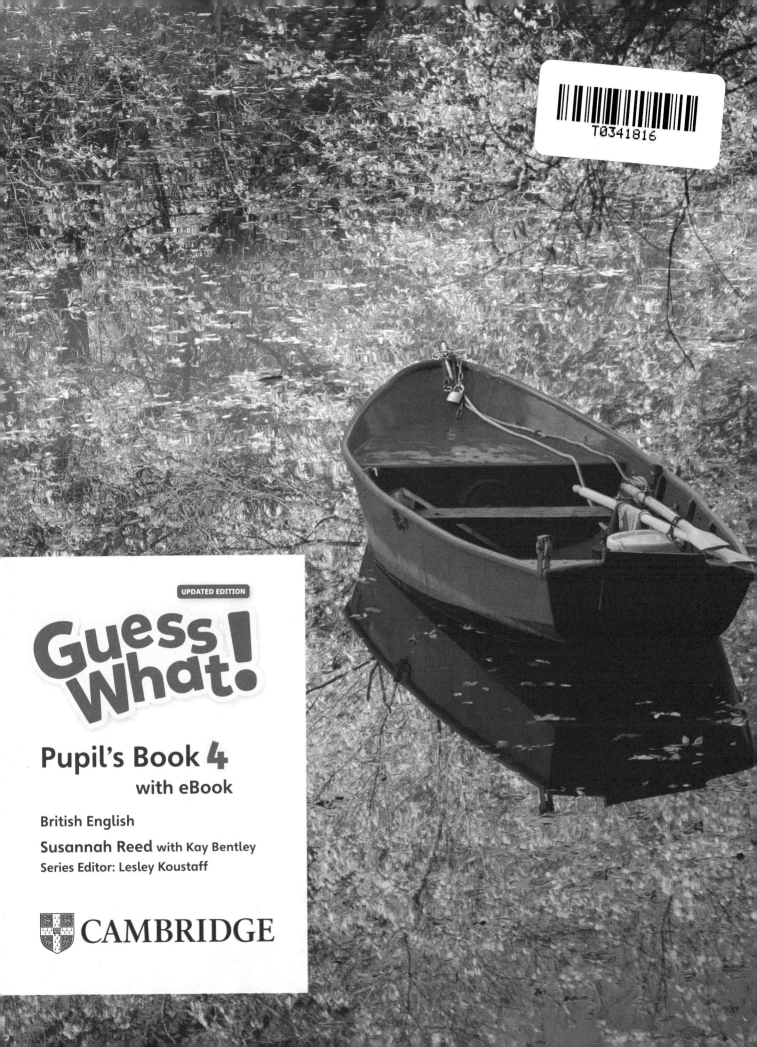

UPDATED EDITION

Guess What!

Pupil's Book 4
with eBook

British English

Susannah Reed with Kay Bentley
Series Editor: Lesley Koustaff

CAMBRIDGE

Contents

Welcome back!

Look!

Guess What!

5

1 🎧 0.01 **Listen and point.**

2 🎧 0.02 **Listen, point and repeat.**

Lucas

Lily

Tom

Max

Anna

3 🎧 0.03 **Listen and say the names.**

4 (Think) **Describe and guess who.**

Is it a girl or a boy?   It's a boy.

Has he got dark hair?   No, he hasn't.

Is it Tom?   Yes, it is.

❶ dark hair
❷ straight hair
❸ glasses
❹ fair hair
❺ curly hair
❻ red hair

→ Activity Book page 4

5 🎧 0.04 **Listen and match. Then sing the song.**

1 What does Fred look like?
He's tall, he's got blue eyes,
And he's got red hair.
He's got short red hair.

2 What does Jane look like?
She's tall, she's got brown eyes,
And she's got straight hair.
She's got long straight hair.

3 What does Paul look like?
He's short, he's got brown eyes,
And he's got dark hair.
He's got short dark hair.

6 **Look at page 6. Read and match.**

1 What does Lucas look like?

a She's tall. She's got long straight hair.

2 What does Lily look like?

b He's short. He's got brown eyes.

3 What does Tom's sister look like?

c He's tall. He's got short fair hair.

4 What does Anna's brother look like?

d She's short. She's got red hair.

7 (About Me) **Think about your family. Ask and answer.**

What does your cousin look like?

She's short and she's got straight dark hair.

Remember!
What does he look like?
He's tall.
He's got blue eyes.

Grammar fun!

8  **Listen and repeat.**

100 cm = 1 m

10 cm   20 cm   30 cm   40 cm   50 cm   60 cm   70 cm   80 cm   90 cm   100 cm

9 **Listen and match. Then ask and answer with a friend.**

a 76 cm

b 1 m 32 cm

c 91 cm

d 1 m 67 cm

e 1 m 19 cm

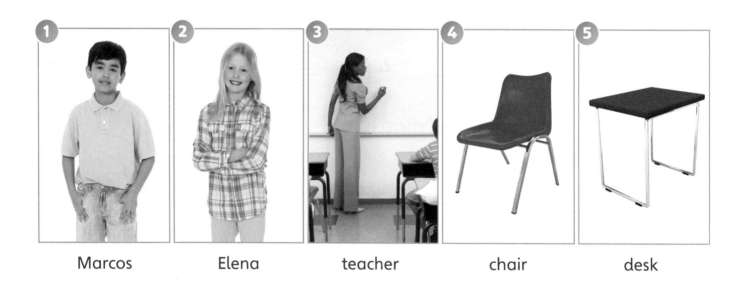

1 Marcos   **2** Elena   **3** teacher   **4** chair   **5** desk

How tall is Marcos?   He's 1 metre 32 centimetres.

How high is the chair?   It's 91 centimetres.

10 **Measure your friends. Then ask and answer.**

How tall are you?   I'm 1 metre 25 centimetres.

> **Remember!**
> 100 centimetres = 1 metre

11 **Go to page 102. Listen and repeat the chant.**

Grammar fun!

Skills: *Reading and speaking*

Let's start! What activities do you do with your friends?

12 🎧 0.08 **Read and listen. Then match.**

My friends

1 My best friend's name is Rosa. She's very tall. She's 1 metre 36 centimetres! She's got long dark hair and brown eyes. We like music and we like playing the recorder together. We have recorder lessons every Wednesday.

2 This is my friend Louis. He's got straight dark hair and green eyes. We're in the same class at school. We like playing table tennis. We play after school on Wednesdays. We like badminton too.

3 This is me with my friends Sally and James. We like horse riding. We have riding lessons on Sundays and we like looking after the horses too. Horses are my favourite animals. They're beautiful.

13 **Read again and answer the questions.**

1 How tall is Rosa?
2 Does Rosa have recorder lessons on Sundays?
3 What does Louis look like?
4 What day do Sally and James go horse riding?

14 **(About Me)** **Think of a friend and answer the questions.**

What's his or her name?
What does he or she look like?
Do you like the same things?
What activities do you do together?

Writing

➡ Activity Book page 7: Write about a friend and what they like doing.

Read and listen. Watch.

Value: Get involved with your local community

→ Activity Book page 8

16   **Listen and repeat. Then act.**

watching TV   going ice skating   making models
playing the guitar   going bowling   playing table tennis

1

What shall we do today?

How about
watching TV?

OK, then.

2

What shall we do today?

How about playing
the guitar?

No, let's
go fishing.

OK, good
idea.

Say it!

17  **Listen and repeat.**

Owls make no sound
when they fly down.

owl

What **patterns** can you **see**?

1 🎧 0.12 **Listen and repeat.**

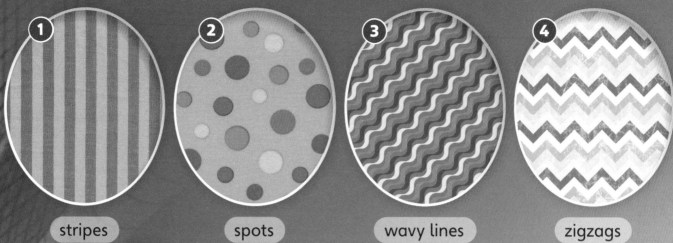

stripes   spots   wavy lines   zigzags

2 CLIL ▶ **Watch the video.**

3 **What patterns can you see in the pictures?**

Guess What!
We all have different patterns of wavy lines on our fingers.

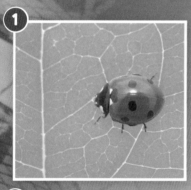

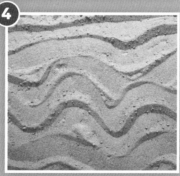

Let's collaborate!

famous   research

discuss   **OUR MAGAZINE INTERVIEW**   choose

interview

Back to School

write

4 **What patterns do you like drawing?**

1 Fun sports

Look!

14

Guess What!

1 🎧 1.01 **Listen and point.**

2 🎧 1.02 **Listen, point and repeat.**

Adventure holidays

1 fishing
2 ice skating
3 skateboarding
4 sailing
5 kayaking
6 bowling
7 mountain biking
8 skiing
9 snowboarding

3 🎧 1.03 **Listen and answer the questions.**

4 (About Me) **Ask and answer with a friend.**

Do you like skiing?   Yes, I do.

5 (1.04) **Listen and choose. Then sing the song.**

1 I'm good at ice skating/mountain biking,
   But I'm not very good at skiing.
   Sally isn't good at ice skating/mountain biking,
   But she's very good at skiing.
   Sally is a good friend,
   But we're good at different things.
   Yes! Sally is a good friend,
   But we're good at different things.

2 I'm good at snowboarding/skateboarding,
   But I'm not very good at sailing.
   Ricky isn't good at snowboarding/
   skateboarding,
   But he's very good at sailing.
   Ricky is a good friend,
   But we're good at different things.
   Yes! Ricky is a good friend,
   But we're good at different things.

6 (About Me) **Make sentences about you and your friends. Say *true* or *false*.**

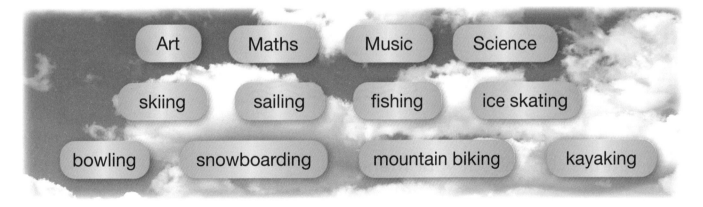

| Art | Maths | Music | Science |

| skiing | sailing | fishing | ice skating |

| bowling | snowboarding | mountain biking | kayaking |

I'm good at bowling.   True!

Juan isn't very   False!
good at ice skating.

Remember!

She's very good at skiing.
I'm not very good at sailing.

Grammar fun!

7 🎧 1.05 **Listen and repeat.**

1 Are you good at skiing?
Yes, I am.
No, I'm not.

2 What are you good at?
I'm good at ice skating.

8 Think **Look and choose. Then ask and answer with a friend.**

1 2 3
4 5 6
7 8 9

9 **Tell the class about your friend.**

Matthew is good at playing table tennis.

10 🎧 1.06 **Go to page 102. Listen and repeat the chant.**

Remember

Are you good at playing the guitar?
Yes, I am.   No, I'm not.
What are you good at?
I'm good at making films.

Grammar fun!

Grammar

→ Activity Book page 14

Skills: *Listening and speaking*

 Do you like talent shows?

11 (1.07) **Listen and match.**

Forest School Talent Show!
4.30 this afternoon in the school hall.

1 Mel   **2 Kim**   **3 Alex**

a   b   c

12 (1.07) **Listen again and answer the questions.**

1   How old is Mel?
2   Is Kim good at making films?
3   Can Alex play the piano?
4   Who is the winner of the talent show?

13 (About Me) **Plan a talent show with your friends.**

What are you good at?

I'm good at music.
I can play the piano.

I can sing!

Writing

→ Activity Book page 15: Plan a talent show.

15   **Listen and repeat. Then act.**

wash the car   paint a picture   make a film
write a story   make a cake   sing a song

1

Who wants to make a cake?

I do. I'm good at making cakes.

2

Who wants to paint a picture?

I don't. I'm not good at Art.

Say it!

16  **Listen and repeat.**

Royal pythons coil into balls on the soil.

royal python

What type of
body movements
can we make?

1 🎧 1.11 Listen and repeat.

1 turn

2 shake

3 bend

4 stretch

5 kick

2 CLIL ▶ Watch the video.

3 What body movements are the children making in these pictures?

Guess What!
We all make the same body movement when we're happy. We smile.

1

2

3

4

4 What body movements do you make in sport?

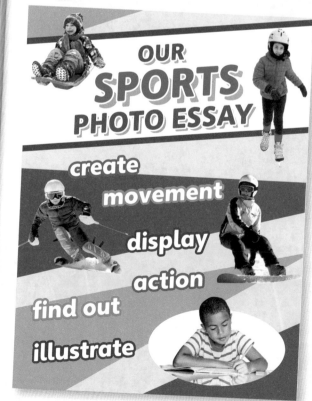

Let's collaborate!

OUR SPORTS PHOTO ESSAY

create
movement
display
action
find out
illustrate

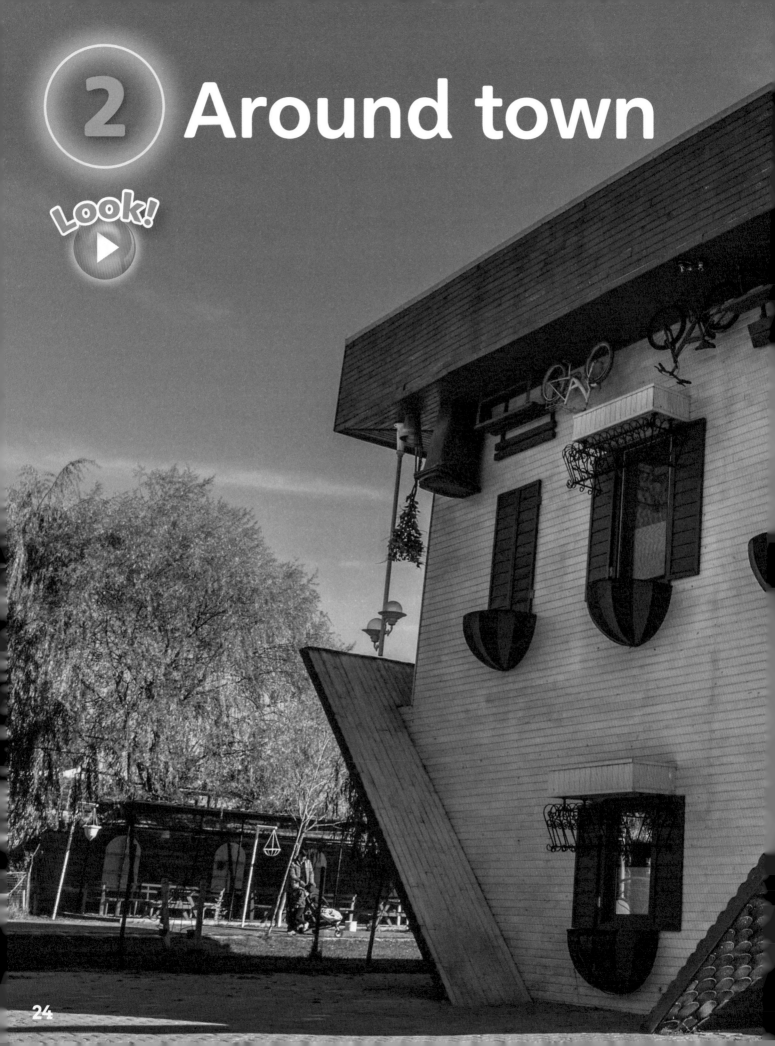

Look!

Guess What!

1 (2.01) **Listen and point.**

2 (2.02) **Listen, point and repeat.**

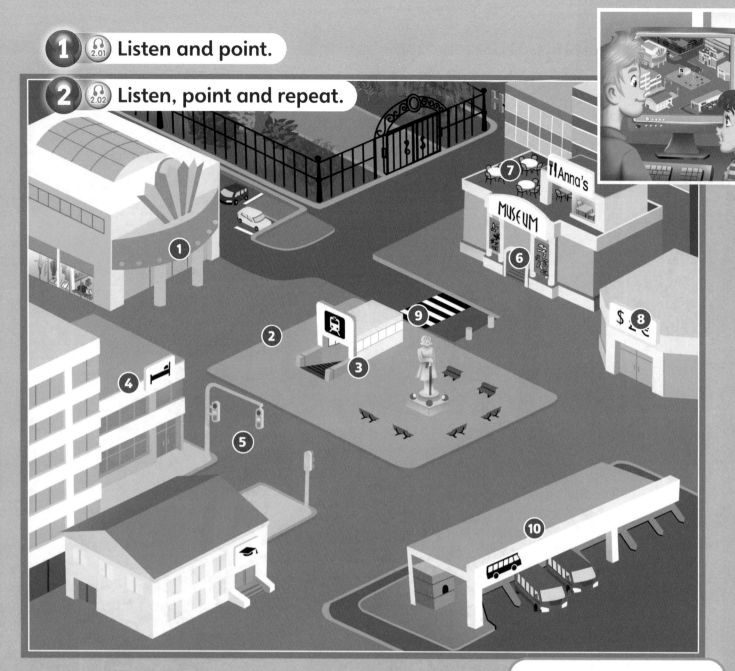

3 (2.03) **Listen and say the words.**

4 (Think) **Look at Tom's map. Describe and guess where.**

It's opposite the park.   Museum!

1 shopping centre
2 square
3 underground station
4 hotel
5 traffic light
6 museum
7 restaurant
8 bank
9 zebra crossing
10 bus station

5 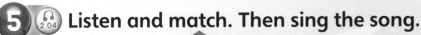 Listen and match. Then sing the song.

1 Where's the museum?
It's in the square.
It's opposite the hotel.
Can you see it over there?

2 Where's the underground station?
It's below the square.
It's near the shopping centre.
Can you see it over there?

3 Where's the plane?
It's above the square.
It's far from the town.
Can you see it up there?

6 Read and match.

1 Where's the museum?

2 Where's the plane?

3 Where's the shopping centre?

4 Where's the underground station?

a It's near the underground station.

b It's below the square.

c It's above the square.

d It's opposite the hotel.

7 (About Me) Make a map of your town. Then ask and answer.

Where's the bank?

It's opposite the school.

No, it isn't! It's next to the museum!

Remember

Where's the bus station?
It's **far from** the hotel.

Grammar fun!

8 **Listen and repeat.**

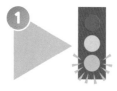

| Start! | Go straight ahead. | Turn left. | Turn right. | Stop! |

9 **Listen and follow. Then answer.**

10 (Think) **Play the game with a friend.**

Start at the restaurant.   Go straight ahead.

11 **Go to page 102. Listen and repeat the chant.**

Remember!
Start at the hotel. Turn right at the library.

Grammar   → Activity Book page 22

Skills: *Reading and speaking*

 What can you see in your town?

12 **Read and listen. Then match.**

My trip to London!

Morning ¹ This is London Zoo. It's really big. It's near my hotel. There are lots of animals in the zoo. This is the giraffe house. Giraffes are my favourite animal.

Lunch ² This is the Rainforest Café. It's my favourite restaurant in London. What can you see behind the tables? They're elephants!

Afternoon ³ This is the Science Museum. And this is my favourite room – the transportation area. There are lots of cars and a lorry. And look above the people. There's a plane!

Evening ⁴ This is Trafalgar Square. There's a big art gallery here. There are statues and a fountain, too.

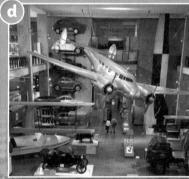

13 **Read again and choose the words.**

1 London Zoo is near/far from his hotel.
2 The Rainforest Café is his favourite shopping centre/restaurant.
3 There's a plane above/below the people in the Science Museum.
4 There's a big art gallery/bus station in Trafalgar Square.

14 (About Me) **Ask and answer with a friend.**

What's your favourite city?
What can you see there?

Writing

➔ Activity Book page 23: Write about your favourite city.

15 🎧 2.09 ▶ Story **Read and listen. Watch.**

1 Week 2 We need nets.

Look at this! A net!

2 Football competition Harton Park How many goals can you score?

Where's Harton?

I know. Follow me.

3 Welcome to Harton

Be careful everyone.

Stop at the traffic lights.

Yes, OK.

4 Excuse me. How do you get to the park?

Turn left at the museum and go straight ahead.

Thanks.

5 Goal!

6 Well done! You're the winners.

Thank you, but we don't need the cup.

7 Can we have the net, please?

It's for the adventure playground.

OK!

30 **Value: Cycle safely**

→ Activity Book page 24

16   **Listen and repeat. Then act.**

library   sports field   shopping centre
supermarket   bus station   dining hall

1

Excuse me. How do you get to the **bus station**?

Turn left at the zebra crossing and go straight ahead.

Thank you.

2

Excuse me. How do you get to the **shopping centre**?

Turn right at the traffic lights and go straight ahead.

Thank you.

Say it!

17 **Listen and repeat.**

Turtles whirl in the surf.

What **3D** **shapes** can you see?

1 (2.12) **Listen and repeat.**

1 sphere   2 cylinder   3 cone   4 cube   5 pyramid

2 CLIL **Watch the video.**

3 **What shapes can you see? Read and match.**

1 This building is a pyramid shape with glass squares.
2 This building is a cube shape.
3 This building has cylinders at the front.
4 This building is a cone shape.
5 This building has a glass sphere on top.

Guess What!
Some Mexican pyramids are 3,000 years old but some Egyptian pyramids are 4,000 years old.

Let's collaborate!

build describe
decide
brainstorm
OUR MODEL TOWN
design
compare

4 **What shapes can you see in buildings near your school?**

Review Units 1 and 2

1 Find the words in the puzzles and match to the photos.

fis

boarding

skate

hing

kaya

arding

snowbo

king

Fred

Alice

Josh

Mia

2 🎧 2.13 Listen and say the names.

3 Answer the questions.

1 Where's Fred?
2 What's Josh good at?
3 Is Mia good at skiing?
4 Is Alice in the square?

4 Make your own word puzzles for your friend.

Choose activities or places in town:
super   urant
resta   market

→ Activity Book pages 28–29

A   B   C   D

1

2

3

SCHOOL

4

MUSEUM

Red

Are you good at (skateboarding)?

Blue

What does he/she look like?

Green

Where's the (bus station)?

Number 1. Letter A.   Are you good at skateboarding?   Yes, I am.

③ At work

Look!
▶

Guess What!

1 🎧 3.01 **Listen and point.**

2 🎧 3.02 **Listen, point and repeat.**

What do people do?

3 🎧 3.03 **Listen and say the words.**

4 (Think) **Describe and guess who.**

She likes helping people.
She's wearing a white coat.

Doctor!

1 doctor
2 nurse
3 artist
4 singer
5 actor
6 vet
7 businessman
8 businesswoman
9 bus driver
10 pilot

5 🎧 3.04 **Listen and choose. Then sing the song.**

1 What does your aunt do? …
She's an artist/singer.
Where does she work? …
She works in a studio.

2 What does your uncle do? …
He's a bus driver/pilot.
Where does he work? …
He works on a plane.

3 What does your cousin do? …
She's a businesswoman/doctor.
Where does she work? …
She works in an office.

6 **Read and match.**

1 My dad's a farmer. He works on a farm.

2 My grandma's a teacher. She works in a school.

3 My mum's a train driver. She works on a train.

4 My grandpa's a doctor. He works in a hospital.

7 **Think about your family. Ask and answer.**

What does your cousin do?

He's a nurse.

Where does he work?

He works in a hospital.

Remember!

What does your aunt do?
She's an artist.
Where does she work?
She works in a studio.

Grammar fun!

8 🎧 3.05 **Listen and repeat.**

1 What do you want to be?

I want to be a footballer.

2 Do you want to be a footballer?

No, I don't. I want to be a singer.

9 (About Me) **Choose what you want to be. Then ask and answer.**

10 **Tell the class about your friend.**

Sally wants to be an actor.

11 🎧 3.06 **Go to page 102. Listen and repeat the chant.**

Remember

What do you want to be?
I want to be a teacher.

Grammar → Activity Book page 32

Skills: *Listening and speaking*

Let's start! **Where do you want to work?**

12 🎧 3.07 **Listen and match.**

Sanjay

a

b

Lola

c

d

13 🎧 3.07 **Listen again and say *true* or *false*.**

1 Sanjay's good at Science.
2 Sanjay wants to be a doctor.
3 Lola wants to work in an office.
4 Lola's good at English.

14 **Ask and answer with a friend.**

What are you good at?
Do you want to work with animals or people?
Do you want to work in a school or in an office?

Writing

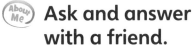 Activity Book page 33: Write about what you want to be and where you want to work.

Listen and repeat. Then act.

give some water to the horse   feed the rabbit   feed the cat
give some milk to the cat   take the dog for a walk

1

Shall I take the dog for a walk?

Yes, please.

2

Shall I feed the cat?

No, thanks, but you can feed the rabbit.

OK.

Say it!

17 Listen and repeat.

Crabs crawl across sand.

crab

What type of
work
is it?

1 🎧 3.11 Listen and repeat.

1 outdoor work   **2** factory work   **3** transport work   **4** shop work

2 CLIL ▶ Watch the video.

3 Look at the pictures. What type of work can you see?

Guess What?
We know how old a tree is from the number of circles in its wood.

Let's collaborate!

discuss   OUR   choose
DREAM JOBS FAIR
write
research   roleplay
ask and answer

4 What types of work do you think are difficult?

Look!

Guess What!

1 (4.01) **Listen and point.**

2 (4.02) **Listen, point and repeat.**

3 (4.03) **Listen and say the animals.**

4 (Think) **Describe and guess what.**

It's brown and it can jump. It's got a long tail.

Kangaroo!

1 kangaroo
2 koala
3 parrot
4 penguin
5 bat
6 owl
7 jaguar
8 bear
9 panda
10 gorilla

5 🎧 4.04 Listen and match. Then sing the song.

1 Gorillas are bigger than pandas,
But gorillas are smaller than bears.
Bears are bigger than gorillas,
And they're bigger than pandas too.
Animals, animals. Look at the animals!

2 Bats are noisier than koalas,
But bats are quieter than parrots.
Parrots are noisier than bats,
And they're noisier than koalas too.
Animals, animals. Look at the animals!

6 Read and say *true* or *false*.

1 Pandas are smaller than bears.
2 Gorillas are bigger than bears.
3 Bears are bigger than pandas.
4 Bats are noisier than parrots.
5 Koalas are quieter than bats.
6 Parrots are quieter than koalas.

7 About Me Make sentences about your favourite animals. Say *true* or *false*.

Tigers are quicker than rabbits.

True!

Remember

bigger
smaller
noisier
quieter

Grammar fun!

8 🎧 4.05 **Listen and repeat.**

1 Are giraffes taller than penguins?

Yes, they are.

2 Are koalas noisier than bears?

No, they aren't.

9 🎧 4.06 **Listen and answer the questions.**

1 small / big

2 tall / short

3 noisy / quiet

4 slow / quick

10 Think **Ask and answer with a friend.**

Are frogs bigger than penguins?   No, they aren't.

11 🎧 4.07 **Go to page 102. Listen and repeat the chant.**

Remember!

Are parrots quieter than rabbits?
Yes, they are.   No, they aren't.

Grammar fun!

Grammar

→ Activity Book page 40

Skills: *Reading and speaking*

Let's start! **Would you like to work in a zoo?**

12 🎧 4.08 **Read and listen. Then match.**

¹ *Meet the squirrel monkeys!*

Squirrel monkeys come from South America. They are small with grey and orange fur. They've got long tails. Squirrel monkeys like fruit, leaves, seeds and insects. They also eat flowers, eggs and small animals. They are good at climbing trees and they are very quick.

² *Meet the wallabies!*

A wallaby looks like a kangaroo but it's smaller. Wallabies come from Australia. They eat grass and plants. Wallabies can't run but they are very good at jumping.

³ *Meet our baby red panda!*

This is Bo. He's our baby red panda! Red pandas come from Asia. They are red and brown and they've got long tails. Red pandas eat lots of things. They like plants, insects, eggs, birds or small animals!

13 **Read again and answer the questions.**

1 Can squirrel monkeys climb trees?
2 What do wallabies eat?
3 Do red pandas eat meat?
4 Which animal comes from Australia?

14 (About Me) **Ask and answer with a friend.**

What's your favourite wild animal?
What does it look like?
Where does it come from?
What does it eat?

Writing

→ Activity Book page 41: Write about your favourite animal.

1 Week 4 We need owl boxes

Are there bird boxes in your garden, Tom?

Yes, there are. But there aren't many.

2

3 No, Anna. We need bigger boxes. Owls are bigger than other birds.

Are these owl boxes?

Let's make one.

4 Grandpa, can you make an owl box for us?

Yes – you can help.

5 Where are the nails?

Here they are.

Can you pass them, please?

6 There you are! A house for an owl!

It's beautiful.

7 Thank you. It's for the nature zone.

Wow! There are lots of boxes.

It's an owl town!

16   **Listen and repeat. Then act.**

kite   rubber   glue   balls   colouring pencils   scissors

1

Where's the glue?

It's here.

Can you pass it, please?

Yes, of course.

2

Where are the scissors?

They're here.

Can you pass them, please?

Yes, of course.

Say it!

17 Listen and repeat.

Frogs catch fruit flies with their tongues.

frog

What animal group is it?

1 🎧 4.12 Listen and repeat.

mammals

reptiles

amphibians

2 CLIL ▶ Watch the video.

3 What animal group is it? Read and match.

1 It's an amphibian. It can live on land and in water.
2 It's a bird and it can fly.
3 It's a fish and it can swim.
4 It's a mammal. It's got spots on it and it can climb.
5 It's a reptile and it can walk and swim.

Guess What! The hummingbird is the only bird that can fly backwards.

4 What group of animals would you like to film?

Let's collaborate!

OUR **ANIMAL** FIELD GUIDE

wild   design

combine

find out

choose

endangered

Review Units 3 and 4

1 **Find the words in the puzzles and match to the photos.**

v*t

p*l*t

s*ng*r

*rt*st

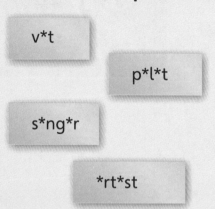

2 **Listen and say the letters.**

(4.13)

3 **Read and answer the questions.**

1 Look at picture a.
   What does she do?

2 Look at picture b.
   Where does she work?

3 Look at picture c.
   Is the sculpture bigger
   or smaller than the artist?

4 Look at picture d.
   Does he work on a plane?

4 **Make your own word puzzles for your friend.**

Choose jobs or wild animals:
k*ng*r**
g*r*ll*

→ Activity Book pages 46–47

Finish

15 tall?

14 vet / zoo?

16 25×3=

13

12 small?

4

5 doctor / hospital?

3 big?

Start

6 quiet?

11 pilot / plane?

2 farmer / office?

1

7

10

9 slow?

8 businessman / studio?

Red
Do you want to be a (doctor)?

Blue
Does (a farmer) work in (an office)?

Yellow
Are (gorillas) (bigger) than (rabbits)?

5 Food and drink

Guess
What!

1 🎧 5.01 **Listen and point.**

2 🎧 5.02 **Listen, point and repeat.**

3 🎧 5.03 **Listen and answer the questions.**

4 Think **Describe and guess who.**

He wants pasta for lunch.   Tom!

❶ pasta
❷ yoghurt
❸ soup
❹ pizza
❺ salad
❻ nuts
❼ tea
❽ coffee
❾ biscuit
❿ crisps

5 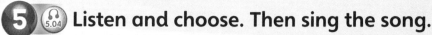 Listen and choose. Then sing the song.

1 I always have a sandwich/pizza for lunch,
And I usually have some fruit.
I sometimes have a yoghurt/soup,
But I never have biscuits or crisps.
No, he never has biscuits or crisps!

2 I usually have pasta/salad for dinner,
And I sometimes have some soup.
I always have some vegetables/fruit,
But I never have biscuits or crisps.
No, he never has biscuits or crisps!

He never has biscuits or crisps!

6 Think Look at the song. Then read and correct the sentences.

1 I never have a sandwich for lunch.
2 I always have pasta for dinner.
3 I sometimes have crisps for lunch.
4 I never have vegetables for dinner.
5 I always have biscuits for dinner.

Number 1. He always has a sandwich for lunch.

always

usually

sometimes

never

7 About Me Make sentences and say *true* or *false*.

I always have crisps for lunch.

False!

Remember!

I always have vegetables for dinner.
He never has biscuits for dinner.

Grammar fun!

8 🎧 5.05 **Listen and repeat.**

How often do you have salad for lunch?

Every day.

Usually.

Sometimes.

Never.

9 (About Me) **Make questions. Then ask and answer with a friend.**

How often
do you have

for breakfast?

for lunch?

for dinner?

10 **Tell the class about you and your friend.**

Pablo has toast for breakfast every day. I usually have yoghurt.

11 🎧 5.06 **Go to page 103. Listen and repeat the chant.**

Remember

How often do you have vegetables for lunch?
Every day. Usually. Sometimes. Never.

Grammar fun!

Skills: *Listening and speaking*

 What do you usually have for lunch?

12 **Listen and match.**

Grace

a

Monday	Tuesday	Wednesday	Thursday
pizza	pasta	soup	sandwich
salad	vegetables	salad	salad
fruit	yoghurt	yoghurt	fruit
yoghurt	water	water	yoghurt
water			water

Louis

b

Monday	Tuesday	Wednesday	Thursday
sandwich	chicken	soup	pasta
salad	salad	salad	vegetables
fruit	fruit	yoghurt	fruit
yoghurt	nuts	fruit	juice
water	juice	water	

13 **Listen again and answer the questions.**

1 How often does Grace have salad for lunch?
2 Does Grace sometimes have pizza?
3 How often does Louis have nuts?
4 Does Louis like yoghurt?

14 (About Me) **Ask and answer with a friend.**

Do you always have a healthy lunch?
Do you usually have fruit, vegetables or salad?
What do you never have for lunch?

Writing

 Activity Book page 51: Make a lunch diary and write about it.

1 Week 5 We need bean bags.

£15! That's a lot of money.

How can we get £15?

£15

2

3 How about selling fruit?

I can give you £10 to buy the fruit.

Thanks, Dad!

4 Let's wash our hands first.

Good idea. Come on, Anna.

OK.

5 We've got fruit salad ...

... and orange juice.

Great!

6 How much is the fruit salad?

It's one pound.

Can I have two, please?

Yes, of course. Here you are.

£1

7 28, 29, 30, 31, 32 pounds. Wow!

We can buy two bean bags!

64   **Value:** Be clean around food

→ Activity Book page 52

16   **Listen and repeat. Then act.**

tea   orange juice   pizza   biscuits   crisps   nuts

1
Extra shot £1.30
Syrup shot £0.25
£0.25

It's one pound.

How much is the orange juice?

Can I have two, please?

Yes, of course.

2
Hot chocolate
Americano £0.75
Fairtrade tea

Speciality teas

How much are the biscuits?

They're fifty pence.

Can I have three, please?

Yes, of course.

Say it!

17 **Listen and repeat.**

Aardvarks come out in the dark.

aardvark

Where does **water** come from?

1 🎧 5.11 Listen and repeat.

rain   glacier   well   spring

2 CLIL ▶ Watch the video.

3 What can you see in the pictures?

4 Where are the big rivers in your country?

Let's collaborate!

buy   OUR   sell

BUSINESS PLAN

count   think about   plan   use money

LEMONADE BAKE SALE

Cakes for Sale

Look!

Guess What!

1 🎧 6.01 **Listen and point.**

2 🎧 6.02 **Listen, point and repeat.**

3 🎧 6.03 **Listen and answer the questions.**

4 (Think) **Describe and guess who.**

He's got a cold.   Tom!

1 cold
2 cough
3 earache
4 stomachache
5 backache
6 sore throat
7 temperature
8 toothache
9 headache

5 🎧 6.04 Listen and match. Then sing the song.

1 Oh dear, what's the matter?
What's the matter with you, Tim?
I've got a headache.
Oh dear, poor you!

2 Oh dear, what's the matter?
What's the matter with Max?
He's got a stomachache.
Oh dear, poor him!

3 Oh dear, what's the matter?
What's the matter with Mary?
She's got a cough and a cold.
Oh dear, poor her!

6 🎧 6.05 Now listen and say the names.

7 Think Play a mime game.

What's the matter with Charlie?

He's got a stomachache.

Have you got a stomachache?

Yes, I have.

Remember

What's the matter?
I've got a cough and a cold.

Grammar fun!

8 🎧 6.06 Listen and repeat.

Can you go sailing today?

No, I can't. I've got a sore throat and a temperature.

9 🎧 6.07 Listen and match.

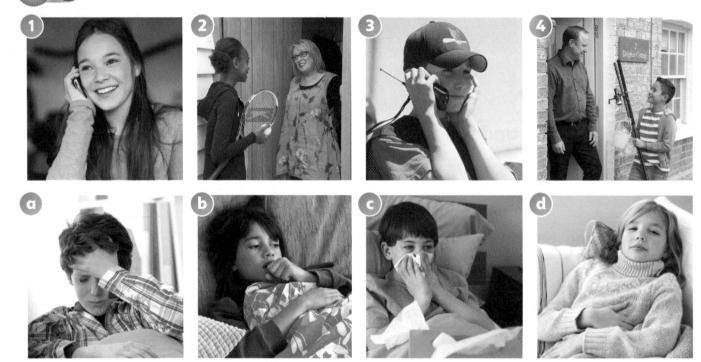

1 2 3 4

a b c d

10 Think Ask questions and say why you can't.

Can you go ice skating today?

No, I can't. I've got an earache.

11 🎧 6.08 Go to page 103. Listen and repeat the chant.

Remember!

Can you play basketball today?
No, I can't. I've got a cough and a cold.

Grammar → Activity Book page 58

Skills: *Reading and speaking*

 How often do you have a cold?

12 🎧 6.09 **Read and listen. Then match.**

Have you got a cold?

Make some lemon and honey! Lemon and honey is a very healthy drink. It's good for colds and it's easy to make! Try this simple recipe at home.

1 You need a lemon, some honey and some hot water.
2 Cut the lemon. Squeeze the juice into a cup.
3 Add some honey.
4 Add the hot water. Be careful! An adult can help.

It's ready! Now sit down and enjoy your lemon and honey!

13 **Read again and say *true* or *false*.**

1 Lemon and honey is a healthy drink.
2 It isn't good for colds.
3 It's difficult to make.
4 You need hot water for the drink.

14 (About Me) **Ask and answer with a friend.**

What healthy food or drinks can you make?
Can you make a salad?
Can you make a fruit salad?
Can you make orange juice?
Can you make a sandwich?

Writing

➡ Activity Book page 59: Write a recipe for a healthy food or drink.

15 6.10 **Story** ▶ **Read and listen. Watch.**

1 Week 6 We need skateboards.

Let's ask our cousin, Chris!

He goes to skateboarding club today.

2

3 skateboarding competition today Win a skateboard!

It's a competition!

Go, Chris!

4 Oh dear!

Are you OK, Chris?

Yes, I think so. My leg hurts, but I'm OK. Don't worry.

5 Have you got a headache, Chris?

No, I'm OK now.

But where's your skateboard?

6 skateboarding compe... today Win a skateboard!

Max!

He's really good!

7 That's OK! I'm good at skateboarding, but Max is very good!

Well done, Max!

Sorry, Chris!

74 **Value:** Be a good sport

→ Activity Book page 60

16 **6.11** **Talk Time** **Listen and repeat. Then act.**

backache   earache   headache   temperature   sore throat   cough

1

Are you OK?

Yes, I think so. Don't worry.

Oh, good!

2

Are you OK?

No, I don't think so. I've got a headache.

Oh dear!

Say it!

17 **6.12** Listen and repeat.

Spiders spin special webs.

spider

What can we use plants for?

1 🎧 6.13 Listen and repeat.

fabric

fuel

medicine

2 CLIL ▶ Watch the video.

3 🎧 6.14 Listen and say what picture it is.

Guess What?
Some bamboo plants can grow almost one metre in a day.

4 Can you think of more things people make with plants?

Let's collaborate!

OUR **PLANT-BASED** PRODUCT

review
create ask and answer

PLANT-BASED OIL

write persuade

brainstorm

Review Units 5 and 6

1 Find the words and match to the photos.

pizzalpastapsaladesoup

2 🎧 6.15 Listen and say the names.

3 Read and say the names.

1 She likes making salad.
2 He sometimes makes pizza.
3 He likes making soup.
4 She often makes pasta with chicken and vegetables.

4 Make your own word puzzle for your friend.

Choose food or health:
toothachebcoughocold

Joe

Will

Rosie

Sara

→ Activity Book pages 64–65

5 **Play the game.**

I never have pizza for breakfast!

How often do you have pasta for dinner? Every day.

7 Buildings

Look!

Guess What!

1 🎧 7.01 **Listen and point.**

2 🎧 7.02 **Listen, point and repeat.**

3 🎧 7.03 **Listen and answer the questions.**

4 Think **Describe and guess where.**

There are lots of old toys here.

Attic!

❶ ground floor	❻	roof
❷ first floor	❼	basement
❸ second floor	❽	garage
❹ third floor	❾	stairs
❺ lift	❿	attic

→ Activity Book page 66

5 🎧 7.04 Listen and choose. Then sing the song.

1 Where were you yesterday?
Where were you yesterday morning?
I was in the kitchen/living room,
In my flat on the second floor.

2 Where were you yesterday?
Where were you yesterday afternoon?
I was in the living room/bedroom,
In my flat on the second floor.

3 Where were you yesterday?
Where were you yesterday evening?
I was in the roof garden/attic,
Above my flat on the second floor.
My flat on the second floor.
The second floor. The second floor.

6 🎧 7.05 Listen and say the names.

John   Marta   Leon   Lola

7 (About Me) Ask and answer with a friend.

Where were you yesterday morning?

I was at home. I was in the living room.

Remember

Where were you yesterday morning?
I was in the kitchen.

Grammar fun!

→ Activity Book page 67   Grammar   83

8  **Listen and repeat.**

Were you at home last night?

No, I wasn't. I was at the cinema.

Yes, I was.

Were you at home?

9 (Think) **Make questions. Ask and answer with a friend.**

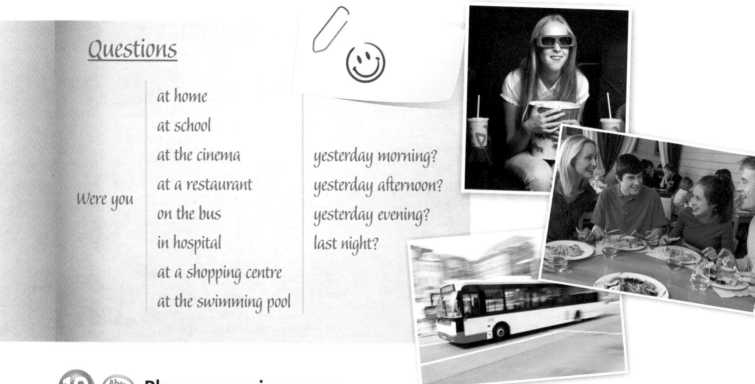

Questions

Were you | at home
at school
at the cinema
at a restaurant
on the bus
in hospital
at a shopping centre
at the swimming pool

yesterday morning?
yesterday afternoon?
yesterday evening?
last night?

10 (About Me) **Play a guessing game.**

Were you in hospital last night?

No, I wasn't. Guess again.

11 **Go to page 103. Listen and repeat the chant.**

Remember

Were you at home last night?
Yes, I was.   No, I wasn't.

 Grammar fun!

84

Grammar

→ Activity Book page 68

Skills: *Listening and speaking*

 Who's your favourite singer?

12 (7.08) **Look at Misha's diary. Listen and choose.**

Misha

Saturday

Morning
at home / in a hotel / at a shopping centre

Lunch
in a restaurant / at home / in a park

Afternoon
at home / in the recording studio / at the cinema

Evening
in a hotel / at home / at a concert

13 (7.08) **Listen again and answer the questions.**

1 Where was Misha in the morning?
2 Where was she at lunch?
3 Where was she in the afternoon?
4 Where was she in the evening?

14 (About Me) **Ask and answer with a friend.**

Where were you on Saturday morning?
Where were you on Sunday afternoon?
Were you at the park on Saturday?
Were you at a concert on Saturday evening?

Writing

 Activity Book page 69: Choose one day. Where were you? Write a diary for that day.

→ Activity Book page 70

Listen and repeat. Then act.

grandpa Ben Jane grandma Lara Uncle John

1

Hello?

Hello, it's Sam. Is Jane there, please?

Yes, she is. Just a minute.

Thank you.

2

Hello?

Hello, it's Sally. Is grandpa there, please?

No, I'm sorry, he isn't.

OK, thank you. Goodbye.

17 7.11 **Listen and repeat.**

Black ducks stand on rocks.

black duck

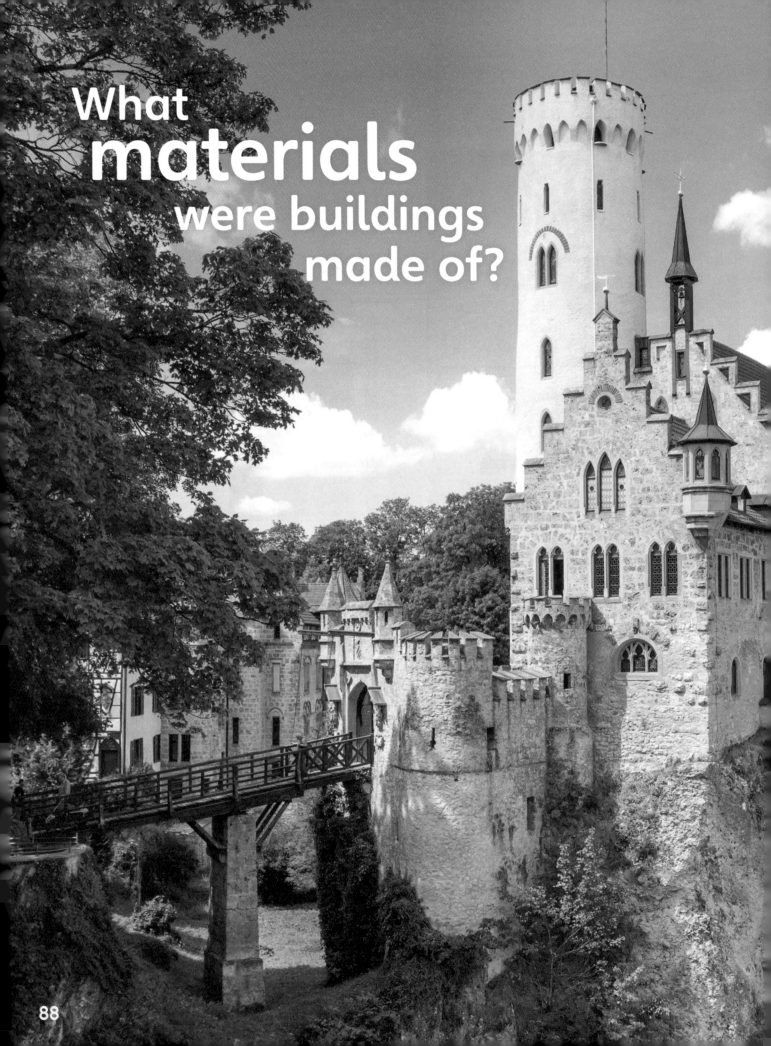

What materials were buildings made of?

1 🎧 7.12 **Listen and repeat.**

1

clay

2

stone

3

animal skins

2 CLIL ▶ **Watch the video.**

3 **What are these buildings made of?**

1
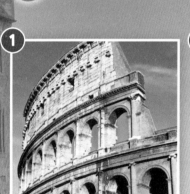

2

3

4

Guess What!
Animal skins were used for water bottles in the eighth century.

4 **What different things are made of stone?**

Let's collaborate!

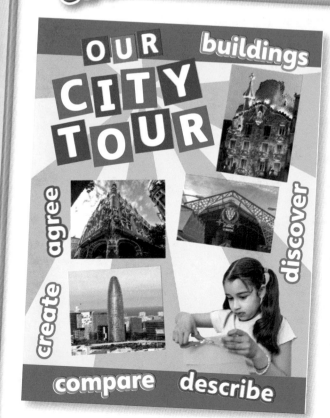

OUR buildings
CITY TOUR
agree discover
create compare describe

→ Activity Book page 72

CLIL: History

8 Weather

Look!

Guess What!

1 🎧 8.01 **Listen and point.**

2 🎧 8.02 **Listen, point and repeat.**

Today's weather

Temperature

Weather

3 🎧 8.03 **Listen and say the numbers.**

4 (About Me) **Ask and answer with a friend.**

Do you like cold weather?   No, I don't. I like hot weather.

1 hot
2 sunny
3 cold
4 warm
5 snowy
6 cloudy
7 foggy
8 windy
9 rainy

→ Activity Book page 74

5 (8.04) Listen and match. Then sing the song.

1 What was the weather like yesterday?
It was cold and rainy.
What's the weather like today?
It's hot and sunny.
Today it's hot and sunny.
So we can go out and play.
Hooray!

2 What was the weather like yesterday?
It was cold and foggy.
What's the weather like today?
It's cold and snowy.
Today it's cold and snowy.
So we can go out and play.
Hooray!

6 (8.05) Listen and answer the questions.

yesterday morning

yesterday afternoon

yesterday evening

last night

7 Think Ask and answer with a friend. Say *true* or *false*.

What was the weather like yesterday?

It was cold and snowy.

False! It was cold and rainy.

Remember!

It was cold and rainy yesterday.
It's hot and sunny today.

Grammar fun!

8 🎧 (8.06) **Listen and repeat.**

1

Was it cloudy on Monday?

No, it wasn't. It was hot and sunny.

2

Was it rainy on Saturday?

Yes, it was.

9 🎧 (8.07) **Look at the weather diary. Listen and answer the questions.**

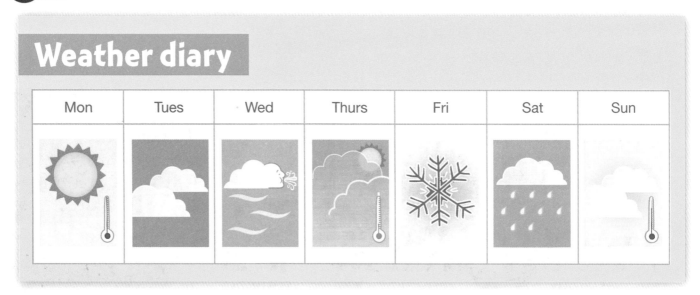

Weather diary

Mon	Tues	Wed	Thurs	Fri	Sat	Sun

10 (About Me) **Make a weather diary. Ask and answer with a friend.**

Was it hot and sunny on Saturday?

No, it wasn't. It was cold and rainy.

11 🎧 (8.08) **Go to page 103. Listen and repeat the chant.**

Remember

Was it hot and sunny on Monday?
Yes, it was.   No, it wasn't.

Grammar fun! ▶

Grammar

→ Activity Book page 76

Skills: *Reading and speaking*

Let's start! **Is it snowy in your country?**

12 🎧 8.09 **Read and listen. Then match.**

Hi Kalu,

1 How are you? I'm fine. It was my birthday on Saturday. I'm eleven now. My birthday was great. It was a cold and snowy day and I was at the Sapporo Snow Festival with my family.

2 The snow festival is every year in February. It's fantastic. It's really big and there are lots of amazing snow sculptures. This is a photo of my favourite snow sculpture this year. Can you see what it is? It's a snow building.

3 There are also snow animals and lots of snowmen and women. This is a snow family!

4 The snow festival is beautiful at night too. What's your favourite festival?

Email me soon.

Best wishes,

Yasuko

13 **Read and say *true* or *false*.**

1 Yasuko's birthday was on Sunday.
2 Yasuko was at the snow festival with her friends.
3 The snow festival is every April.
4 Yasuko likes the snow festival.
5 You can see lots of snow sculptures at the festival.

14 **About Me** **Ask and answer with a friend.**

When's your birthday?
What festivals do you have in your country?
What's your favourite festival?

Writing

➡ Activity Book page 77: Write about your favourite festival.

1 Adventure Playground

Well done, everyone! Our adventure playground is ready! Please come to the opening party on Saturday at four o'clock.

2

It's Saturday today!

What time does the party start?

At four o'clock.

Hurry up, we're late!

3 Adventure Playground

Welcome, everyone, and thank you for your hard work!

I want to be on TV!

4

The adventure playground is now open!

5

Wow! This is fantastic.

Quicker!

Look! There's an owl.

Value: Work hard and try your best

→ Activity Book page 78

16   **Listen and repeat. Then act.**

TV programme   talent show   film   snow festival
birthday party   swimming competition

1
When does the film start?

At five o'clock.

Hurry up! We're late.

2
What time does the birthday party start?

OK, we have time.

At half past seven.

Say it!

17   **Listen and repeat.**

Elands eat grass and are land animals.

eland

What's the **weather** like around the **world?**

1 🎧 8.13 Listen and repeat.

1 hurricane 2 tornado 3 rainstorm 4 blizzard 5 thunder and lightning

2 CLIL ▶ Watch the video.

3 What's the weather like? Read and match.

1 This weather's snowy and very cold.
2 It's a cone-shaped storm above the land.
3 This weather's cloudy and very rainy.
4 After we see this, it's very noisy.
5 It goes above the sea, then on the land. It's got an eye.

Guess What! The middle of a hurricane is called its eye.

4 What type of weather would you like to write about in a story?

Let's collaborate!

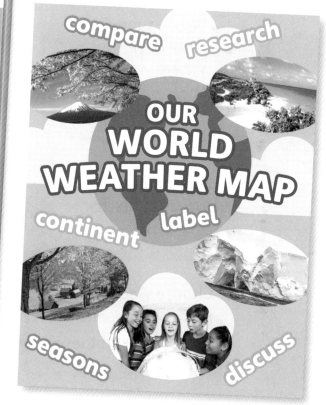

compare research OUR WORLD WEATHER MAP continent label seasons discuss

Review Units 7 and 8

1 Find the words and match to the photos.

ysown

nusny

yiran

dinwy

2 🎧 8.14 Listen and say the letters.

3 Read and answer.

  1 Look at picture a. What was the weather like?

  2 Look at picture b. Was it sunny?

  3 Look at picture c. Where was she?

  4 Look at picture d. Was he at the beach?

4 Make your own word puzzles for your friend.

Choose weather or places in a building:
orof tiasrs mbtaense

→ Activity Book pages 82–83

5 **Play the game.**

Yesterday at half past twelve …

Player 1
1 Was it windy?
2 Was it hot?
3 Where was the cat?
4 Where was the gorilla?
5 Was the bike in the garage?
6 Was Lucy in the attic?

Player 2
1 Was it snowy?
2 Was it cold?
3 Where was the dog?
4 Where was the penguin?
5 Was the parrot in the kitchen?
6 Was Miles in the basement?

Chants

Welcome back! (page 8)

 Listen and repeat the chant.

Ten, twenty, thirty,
Forty, fifty, sixty,
Seventy, eighty, ninety
And one hundred!
I can count to one hundred.

Ten, twenty, thirty,
Forty, fifty, sixty,
Seventy, eighty, ninety
And one hundred!
I can count to one hundred.

Unit 1 (page 18)

 Listen and repeat the chant.

Are you good at skiing?
Yes, I am. Yes, I am.
What are you good at?
I'm good at skiing.

Are you good at ice skating?
No, I'm not. No, I'm not.
What are you good at?
I'm good at roller skating.

Unit 2 (page 28)

 Listen and repeat the chant.

Start at the traffic lights!
Go straight ahead.
Turn left at the bank.
Stop! Stop! Stop!

Start at the traffic lights!
Go straight ahead.
Turn right at the park.
Stop! Stop! Stop!

Unit 3 (page 40)

 Listen and repeat the chant.

What do you want to be?
I want to be a singer.
Do you want to be a singer?
Yes, I do. Yes, I do.

Do you want to be a teacher?
No, I don't. No, I don't.
I want to be a doctor.
George wants to be a doctor.

Unit 4 (page 50)

 Listen and repeat the chant.

Are giraffes taller than penguins?
Yes, they are. Yes, they are.
Are koalas noisier than bears?
No, they aren't. No, they aren't.

Are snakes longer than crocodiles?
Yes, they are. Yes, they are.
Are frogs bigger than owls?
No, they aren't. No, they aren't.

Unit 5 (page 62)

 Listen and repeat the chant.

How often do you have salad for lunch?
Every day. Every day.
I have salad for lunch every day.
He has salad for lunch every day.

How often do you have toast for breakfast?
Never. Never. Never.
I never have toast for breakfast.
She never has toast for breakfast.

Unit 6 (page 72)

 Listen and repeat the chant.

Can you go sailing today?
No, I can't. No, I can't.
I've got a sore throat and a temperature.
Oh dear! A sore throat and a temperature.

Can you play basketball today?
No, I can't. No, I can't.
I've got a cough and a cold.
Oh dear! A cough and a cold.

Unit 7 (page 84)

 Listen and repeat the chant.

Were you at home last night?
Yes, I was. Yes, I was.
I was at home.

Were you at home last night?
No, I wasn't. No, I wasn't.
I was at the cinema.

Unit 8 (page 94)

 Listen and repeat the chant.

Was it hot and sunny on Monday?
Yes, it was. Yes, it was.
It was hot and sunny.

Was it hot and sunny on Tuesday?
No, it wasn't. No, it wasn't.
It was cloudy.

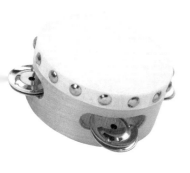

Acknowledgements

Many thanks to everyone in the excellent team at Cambridge University Press & Assessment in Spain, the UK and India.

The authors and publishers would like to thank the following contributors:

Blooberry Design: concept design, cover design, book design
Hyphen: publishing management, page make-up
Ann Thomson: art direction
Gareth Boden: commissioned photography
Jon Barlow: commissioned photography
Ian Harker: class audio recording
Sounds like Mike Ltd: 'Grammar fun' recording
Robert Lee, Dib Dib Dub Studios: song and chant composition
Vince Cross: theme tune composition
James Richardson: arrangement of theme tune
Phaebus: 'CLIL' video production
Kiki Foster: 'Look!' video production
Bill Smith Group: 'Grammar fun' and story animations

The authors and publishers acknowledge the following sources of copyright material and are grateful for the permissions granted. While every effort has been made, it has not always been possible to identify the sources of all the material used, or to trace all copyright holders. If any omissions are brought to our notice, we will be happy to include the appropriate acknowledgements on reprinting and in the next update to the digital edition, as applicable.

Key: U = Unit, Emt = End matter

Photography

The following images are sourced from Getty Images:

U0: Somsak Bumroongwong/EyeEm; FG Trade/E+; Cimmerian/E+; Jose Luis Pelaez Inc/DigitalVision; kyoshino/E+; exxorian/DigitalVision Vectors; Westend61; Gerardo Ricardo López/Moment Open; JohnnyGreig/iStock/Getty Images Plus; Monashee Frantz/OJO Images; sad444/iStock/Getty Images Plus; Imgorthand/E+; Daniel A. Leifheit/Moment; Denis Dumoulin/500px; JBryson/iStock/Getty Images Plus; subjob/iStock/Getty Images Plus; David Kenny/iStock/Getty Images Plus; **U1:** Daniel Milchev/The Image Bank; mbbirdy/E+; Sebastian Condrea/Moment; Imgorthand/E+; Portra/DigitalVision; Ascent Xmedia/Stone; Sean Justice/The Image Bank; Nikoncharly/iStock/Getty Images Plus; Digital Vision/Photodisc; David Cayless; David Kenny/iStock/Getty Images Plus; Arianna Tarenzi/EyeEm; perkmeup/iStock/Getty Images Plus; J and J Productions/Photodisc; Chris Stein/DigitalVision; Michi B; **U2:** Katsumi Murouchi/Moment; frytka/E+; Tom Werner/DigitalVision; anilyanik/DigitalVision Vectors; Jasenka Arbanas/Moment; Richard Sharrocks/Moment; NurPhoto; Jeremy Walker/Stone; leonmoran/iStock/Getty Images Plus; mihtiander/iStock/Getty Images Plus; Mauricio Handler/Photodisc; View Pictures/Universal Images Group; Michael DeYoung/Tetra images; **U3:** Morsa Images/DigitalVision; Digital Vision/Photodisc; FatCamera/E+; Pawita Warasiri/EyeEm; Nathan Bilow/Photodisc; Simon GRATIEN/Moment; GABRIEL BOUYS/AFP; fototrav/E+; Klaus Vedfelt/DigitalVision; mihtiander/iStock/Getty Images Plus; RainervonBrandis/E+; Philip Dumas/Moment; Maskot; Leonardo Laschera/EyeEm; rusm/iStock/Getty Images Plus; MLADEN ANTONOV/AFP; **U4:** letty17/E+; Biswadip Ghosh/500px; Ekaterina Goncharova/Moment; Lezh/E+; Foodcollection; Alistair Berg/Stone; Frans Lemmens/Corbis Unreleased; UpperCut Images; CreativeNature_nl/iStock/Getty Images Plus; Mike Powles/Stone; Oli Scarff/Getty Images News; jordieasy/iStock/Getty Images Plus; Marianne Purdie/Moment; QueGar3/iStock/Getty Images Plus; szefei/iStock/Getty Images Plus; annick vanderschelden photography/Moment; C Flanigan/FilmMagic; Hugo Ortu±o Sußrez/Moment; 1001nights/E+; **U5:** Roberto A Sanchez/E+; pagadesign/E+; twomeows/Moment; Ivan Negru/500px; Carbonero Stock/Moment; Image Source; rudisill/E+; clubfoto/iStock/Getty Images Plus; Weekend Images Inc./iStock/Getty Images Plus; David Papazian/Corbis; David Cayless; AB Photography/iStock/Getty Images Plus; Paul Souders/Stone; Roberto Moiola/Sysaworld/Moment; somnuk krobkum/Moment; energyy/iStock/Getty Images Plus; **U6:** trigga/E+; GYRO PHOTOGRAPHY/amana images; Paolo Negri/Photographer's Choice; Jacky Parker Photography/Moment; Ekaterina Goncharova/Moment; Eskay Lim/EyeEm; enjoynz/DigitalVision Vectors; Andersen Ross Photography Inc/DigitalVision; Catherine Falls Commercial/Moment; Fabrice LEROUGE/ONOKY; BSIP/Collection Mix: Subjects; chameleonseye/iStock/Getty Images Plus; Klaus Vedfelt/DigitalVision; szefei/iStock/Getty Images Plus; jokuephotography/iStock/Getty Images Plus; John Elk III/The Image Bank Unreleased; Westend61; Andersen Ross/Photodisc; Luca Silvestro Santilli/EyeEm;

Paul Viant/iStock/Getty Images Plus; **U7:** Shaun Egan/The Image Bank; MOF/E+; Cultura Exclusive/Quim Roser/Image Source; Â©fitopardo/Moment; FOTOGRAFIA INC./E+; Coal Photography/Alexander Legaree/Moment; Jupiterimages/Stockbyte; kali9/iStock/Getty Images Plus; Birgid Allig/Corbis; Daniel A. Leifheit/Moment; KathyKafka/iStock/Getty Images Plus; imetlion/iStock/Getty Images Plus; **U8:** Peerakit Jirachetthakun/Moment; Buena Vista Images/Photodisc; Ron and Patty Thomas/E+; Jack Pan/500px/500Px Plus; moodboard/Brand X Pictures; Ron Evans/Stockbyte; Sungmoon Han/EyeEm; Wang Zhaobo/VCG; YOSHIKAZU TSUNO/Gamma-Rapho; wisarut_ch/Shutterstock; anmbph/iStock/Getty Images Plus; Wan Ru Chen/Moment; Warren Faidley/The Image Bank; Cultura RM Exclusive/Jason Persoff Stormdoctor/Image Source; Manuel Peric/EyeEm; V_Sot/iStock/Getty Images Plus; John Sirlin/EyeEm; Aaron Horowitz/The Image Bank; Alistair Berg/DigitalVision; Stockbyte; benedektibor/iStock/Getty Images Plus.

The following images are sourced from other libraries:

U0: Tatiana Popova/Shutterstock; View Stock/Alamy; Bejim/Shutterstock; ESB Professional/Shutterstock; Kuttig - People/Alamy Stock Photo; Image navi - Sozaijiten/Alamy; Thierry GRUN/Alamy; Daniela Pelazza/Shutterstock; MT511/Shutterstock; irin-k/Shutterstock; Moiz Husein Dossaji/Shutterstock; Jirik V/Shutterstock; **U1:** Pakhnyushchy/Shutterstock; Lora liu/Shutterstock; Mira/Alamy; Image Source Plus/Alamy; Radius Images/Design Pics/Alamy; Amy Myers/Shutterstock; David & Micha Sheldon/F1online digitale Bildagentur GmbH/Alamy; **U2:** QQ7/Shutterstock; Greg Williams/Shutterstock; Michael Kemp/Alamy; yuanyuan xie/Zoonar GmbH/Alamy; Dan Kosmayer/Shutterstock; Laborant/Shutterstock; gmstockstudio/Shutterstock; popartic/Shutterstock; KULISH VIKTORIIA/Shutterstock; Joseph Sohm/Shutterstock; Elnur Amikishiyev/Shutterstock; Sergio Bertino/Shutterstock; Styve Reineck/Shutterstock; Denis Radovanovic/Shutterstock; tab62/Shutterstock; **U3:** StockLite/Shutterstock; Juice Images272/Alamy; V.S.Anandhakrishna/Shutterstock; Belikova Oksana/Shutterstock; Lumi images/Alamy; lunamarina/Shutterstock; Monkey Business Images/Shutterstock; Grzegorz Petrykowski/Shutterstock; Leandro Mise/Alamy; Lloyd Sutton/Alamy; Steve Arnold/Alamy; **U4:** Milosz Maslanka/Shutterstock; Jl de Wet/Shutterstock; Ryan M. Bolton/Shutterstock; Anton_Ivanov/Shutterstock; Subbotina Anna/Shutterstock; Media Home/Shutterstock; Cathy Keifer/Shutterstock; Ricardo Canino/Shutterstock; Johan Swanepoel/Shutterstock; subin pumsom/Shutterstock; paytai/Shutterstock; Matt Jeppson/Shutterstock; reptiles4all/Shutterstock; Bill Kennedy/Shutterstock; Dirk Ercken/Shutterstock; Audrey Snider-Bell/Shutterstock; Mikadun/Shutterstock; Jean-Edouard Rozey/Shutterstock; Jim Pickerell/Stock Connection Blue/Alamy; **U5:** Nitr/Shutterstock; triocean/Shutterstock; page frederique/Shutterstock; M. Unal Ozmen/Shutterstock; Lestertair/Shutterstock; Africa Studio/Shutterstock; papkin/Shutterstock; Alessio Orru/Shutterstock; Reika/Shutterstock; Suprun Vitaly/Shutterstock; nito/Shutterstock; Marina Grau/Shutterstock; the stock company/Shutterstock; sondem/Shutterstock; Gerhard Zwerger-Schoner/imageBROKER.com GmbH & Co. KG/Alamy; Stephen Coyne/Art Directors/Alamy; Denis Kichatof/Shutterstock; peresanz/Shutterstock; **U6:** Bob Mitchell/Corbis; Radius Images/Design Pics/Alamy; Irina Mos/Shutterstock; Malivan_luliia/Shutterstock; Lifestyle Travel Photo/Shutterstock; Destinyweddingstudio/Shutterstock; Mikhail Pozhenko/Shutterstock; Denis Tabler/Shutterstock; tristan tan/Shutterstock; Russel Wasserfall/Gallo Images/Alamy; Antonova Ganna/Shutterstock; Elly Godfroy/Alamy; Alexandr Makarov/Shutterstock; Africa Studio/Shutterstock; my nordic/Shutterstock; **U7:** Gallo Images - LKIS/Alamy; Khakimullin Aleksandr/Shutterstock; Monkey Business Images/Shutterstock; Christian Mueller/Shutterstock; balabolka/Shutterstock; Andre Babiak/Alamy; dwphotos/Shutterstock; Sasa Komlen/Shutterstock; MORANDI Bruno/hemis.fr/Alamy; Pecold/Shutterstock; Ragnar Th Sigurdsson/ARCTIC IMAGES/Alamy; saras66/Shutterstock; kosmos111/Shutterstock; David South/Alamy; **U8:** Robert Postma/All Canada Photos/Alamy; icollection/Alamy; Cal Vornberger/Alamy; nodff/Shutterstock; stock_shot/Shutterstock; wisarut_ch/Shutterstock; peresanz/Shutterstock; Jim Reed/Jim Reed Photography - Severe&/Corbis; Gregory Pelt/Shutterstock; Igumnova Irina/Shutterstock; Adrian Sherratt/Alamy; blue67design/Shutterstock; Elena Schweitzer/Shutterstock.

Front cover Photography

Front Cover photography by Roman Pretot/500px.

Illustrations

A Corazon Abierto (Sylvie Poggio Artists); Luke Newell; Marcus Cutler (Sylvie Poggio Artists); Pablo Gallego.